# HOW MANY
# BABY PANDAS?

## SANDRA MARKLE

Walker & Company
New York

# How many baby pandas have just been born?

**1 ONE**

At birth, a baby giant panda is only about 6 inches (15 centimeters) long and weighs about 4 ounces (113 grams).

A baby giant panda develops for about 160 days. So when it is born, it's tiny—about the size of a hot dog! It is also blind, nearly bare—with just a thin coat of white hair—and helpless.

In the wild, a mother panda gives birth in a *den*, like a hollow tree or a cave. To move her baby, she gently picks it up in her mouth. When she stops, she holds her baby against her chest so it can *nurse*, feeding on the milk she produces.

Sometimes, though, mother pandas have two babies—twins.

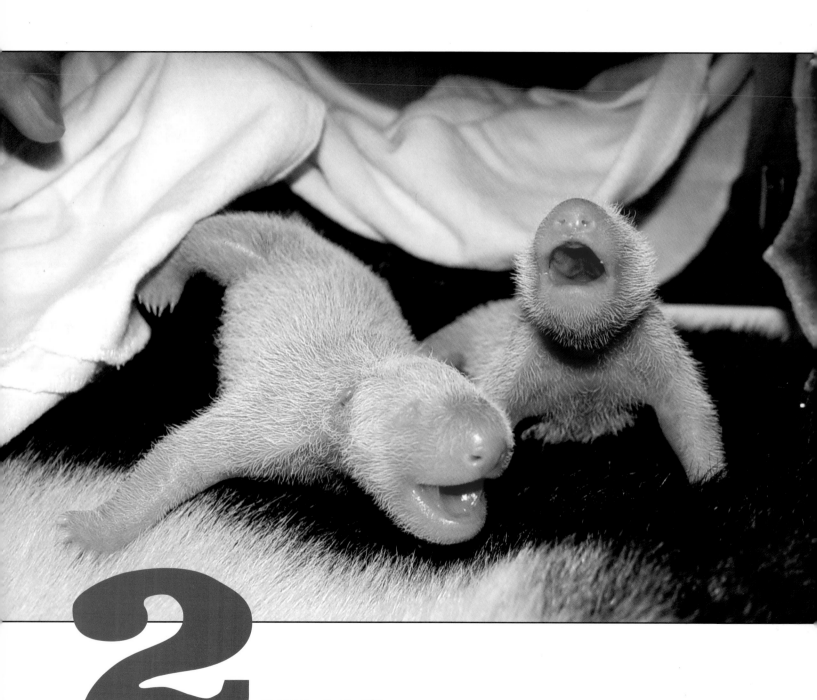

2 TWO

For about the first two months, a baby giant panda needs a lot of its mother's time. It needs to nurse as many as eight times a day. It also needs to be held to stay warm. Taking care of her baby makes it hard for a mother panda to eat or rest enough. So a wild mother panda can care for only one baby.

In the forests of China, where wild giant pandas live, the other twin usually dies. But in zoos and China's Wolong Giant Panda Breeding Center, the other baby is placed in an *incubator* — a machine to keep it warm. Human keepers feed and clean it. At the end of each week, the twins are swapped so each spends time with its mother.

How many baby pandas are taking a nap?

# 3

## THREE

Baby giant pandas, like human babies, sleep a lot. Most of their energy goes toward growing bigger. They also grow their fur coat. Then they can stay warm on their own.

**When baby giant pandas are about two months old, their eyes open.**

How
many
panda
cubs are
climbing?

4
**FOUR**

When baby giant pandas are three to four months old, they start to crawl. By five months, they can climb. If the *cub* gets afraid or hungry, it squeals loudly. Then Mom comes to the rescue.

How
many
baby
pandas
are
eating?

5

**FIVE**

# How many baby pandas are playing?

**6**
**SIX**

**Three on the playground . . .**

Baby giant pandas need their mother's milk for about eighteen months. As they get older and bigger, they nurse longer but less often. For baby giant pandas not being fed by their mothers, zoos mix up a creamy milk substitute. The babies drink this from bottles, or they lap it out of bowls.

# ... plus three in the yard.

In the wild, a cub's only playmate is its mother. At the Wolong Center, the cubs have lots of playmates.

# How many panda cubs are chewing bamboo?

7 SEVEN

From the time they are young, giant panda cubs chew on *bamboo*. They do this because it's what Mom does.

Their baby teeth aren't strong enough for them to eat bamboo. They mainly play with the *stalks*. This way they learn to use their special wristbone like a thumb.

In the wild, giant pandas sit in a patch of bamboo and bend or break the tough bamboo stalks to reach the leaves.

# How many panda cubs are resting?

8 EIGHT

At about a year old, giant panda cubs get their adult teeth and start eating bamboo. Bamboo does not supply a lot of energy, though. So pandas must spend as many as fourteen hours a day eating. No wonder they need to nap between meals!

The giant panda is one of the few animals that eats bamboo.

# How many baby pandas live wild and free?

**Not enough.**
**Hopefully one day, with help from people, there will be lots more.**

A giant panda cub stops nursing when it is about eighteen months old. The mother will not have another baby until her cub is at least two years old. Then, she will mate in the spring, if she can find a male.

In the past, that was not a problem. Today, fewer than 1,600 pandas remain in the wild. They live only in China, in forests that are far apart. So finding a mate isn't easy.

That explains why female pandas usually raise no more than eight babies in a lifetime.

**Giant pandas make sounds and give off scents to find a mate.**

The biggest problem for giant pandas is that the forests where they live are being cleared. To help, the Chinese government is keeping some forests safe just for giant pandas. People are not allowed to live there or cut down the trees.

Zoos and special breeding centers are also raising giant panda cubs. The goal is to release young pandas into the forests.

# Giant Pandas Are Cool!

🐾 Giant pandas are a kind of bear. To help them chew tough bamboo, they have bigger jaw muscles than other kinds of bears. Because of the way these muscles attach to their skulls, their ears wiggle when they chew.

🐾 By the time a giant panda is full grown, it is about 5 feet (1.5 meters) long and weighs more than 200 pounds (91 kilograms). That's about 800 times bigger than when it was born!

🐾 It snows in the winter where giant pandas live. But the panda's coat keeps it warm and dry. It is made up of two layers: long outer hairs and short, woolly underfur.

🐾 Adult pandas usually live alone. Each has a home range, an area where it lives and finds enough bamboo to eat. A female's may be as small as 100 acres (about 40 hectares). A male's is usually bigger. Its home range overlaps the home ranges of several females, with whom it mates. When a cub leaves its mother, it travels until it can settle in an area not already claimed by another giant panda.

# Glossary/Index

# The Wolong Giant Panda Breeding Center

Started in the early 1980s, this was one of the earliest panda research centers established in China. It's in the Wolong Nature Reserve, which was set aside to preserve the giant panda's wild habitat. This center has been a leader in both breeding and caring for giant pandas. Its goal is to increase the giant panda population and to return pandas to their natural habitat.

# Where Giant Pandas Live

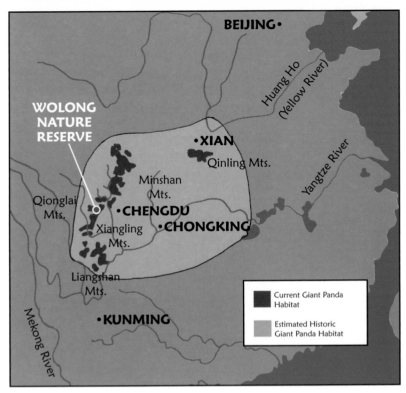

Look at this map to see where giant pandas live in the wild. They once ranged over southern and eastern China, North Vietnam, and Myanmar (Burma). Now they live in only a limited number of forested areas in China.

# Author's Note

On May 5, 2008, a strong (7.9 magnitude) earthquake struck very close to the Wolong Giant Panda Breeding Center. Fourteen of the thirty-two buildings housing the pandas were destroyed, and the others were severely damaged. Sadly, several staff members and one panda were killed. Other staff members and two pandas suffered minor injuries. The rest of the nearly sixty pandas, including fourteen cubs born the previous year, were completely fine. Emergency food supplies were rushed to Wolong, so the pandas were able to remain safe and well cared for.

Today, some of the pandas have been moved to zoos to reduce the risk to the breeding population. However, plans to rebuild Wolong are underway. To find out more about what is happening at Wolong and how your family can help the giant pandas, visit the following Web sites: Smithsonian National Zoological Park "Working Hard to Help the Pandas" (http://nationalzoo.si.edu/Forms/GPDonation/default.cfm) or Michigan State University "Help Panda" (http://www.csis.msu.edu/help/donation.htm). Donations may also be sent to the Panda Mountain-U.S.-China Environmental Fund, 3422 Kelliher Road, Mount Horeb, Wisconsin 53572-1038.

# Digging Deeper

To learn even more about giant pandas, check out these sources.

## BOOKS

Fitzsimons, Cecilia. *Giant Pandas Eat All Day Long* (I Didn't Know That). Brookfield, CT: Copper Beech Books, 2000.
Find out lots of facts about these amazing animals.

Levine, Michelle. *Giant Pandas* (Pull Ahead Books). Minneapolis: Lerner, 2006.
Learn myths and folklore about giant pandas. Then find out more about how this animal lives and efforts to protect it.

Ryder, Joanne. *Little Panda: The World Welcomes Hua Mei at the San Diego Zoo*. New York: Aladdin, 2004.
Follow one baby giant panda growing up at the San Diego Zoo.

## WEB SITES

**San Diego Zoo: Giant Panda News**
http://www.sandiegozoo.org/news/panda_news.html
Learn how the baby pandas at the zoo changed as they grew up.

**Smithsonian National Zoological Park: Giant Pandas** http://nationalzoo.si.edu/Animals/GiantPandas/
The live panda cams are a fun way to see real giant pandas in action. Don't miss the "Giant Pandas for Kids" link to fun activities.

**Zoo Atlanta: Panda Cam**
http://www.zooatlanta.org/animals_panda_cam.php4
See live images of the zoo's giant panda. Then follow links to learn about the zoo's resident pandas, facts about giant pandas, and conservation efforts to save giant pandas in their home range.

# FOR CURIOUS KIDS EVERYWHERE

**Acknowledgments:** For sharing their expertise and enthusiasm, I would especially like to thank Dr. Jianguo (Jack) Liu, Michigan State University; Dr. Rebecca Snyder, Zoo Atlanta; Marc Brody, U.S.–China Environmental Fund (USCEF); and Lisa Stevens, the Smithsonian National Zoo. A special thank-you to Skip Jeffery for his support throughout the creative process.

---

First published in the United States of America in 2009 by Walker Publishing Company, Inc.
Visit Walker & Company's Web site at www.walkeryoungreaders.com

For information about permission to reproduce selections from this book, write to
Permissions, Walker & Company, 175 Fifth Avenue, New York, New York 10010

Library of Congress Cataloging-in-Publication Data
Markle, Sandra.
How many baby pandas? / by Sandra Markle.
p.    cm.
ISBN-13: 978-0-8027-9783-4  •  ISBN-10: 0-8027-9783-0 (hardcover)
ISBN-13: 978-0-8027-9784-1  •  ISBN-10: 0-8027-9784-9 (reinforced)
1. Giant panda—Juvenile literature. 2. Counting—Juvenile literature. I. Title.
QL737.C27M3452 2009          599.789—dc22          2008013321

Typeset in Lino Letter
Book design by Nicole Gastonguay

Printed in China
2  4  6  8  10  9  7  5  3  1  (hardcover)
2  4  6  8  10  9  7  5  3  1  (reinforced)

---

**Photo Credits**
Jessie Cohen, Smithsonian National Zoo **9**
Katherine Feng—Globio—Minden Pictures **2, 3, 5, 6 (top), 7, 11, 12, 13, 16**
Skip Jeffery **23**
Frans Lanting—Minden Pictures **17**
Cyril Ruoso, Minden Pictures **18**
Keren Su, China Span **15, 19**
Xiao Wang, Corbis **14**
Li Wei, China Foto Press **cover, 1, 4, 6 (bottom), 8, 10, 20–21**